essentials

Moving House with Feng Shui

Time-saving books that teach specific skills to busy people, focusing on what really matters; the things that make a difference – the *essentials*. Other books in the series include:

Sell Your Home Using Feng Shui

Writing Good Reports

Speaking in Public

Responding to Stress

Succeeding at Interviews

Solving Problems

Hiring People

Getting Started on the Internet

Writing Great Copy

Making the Best Man's Speech

Making Great Presentations

Making the Most of Your Time

For full details please send for a free copy of the latest catalogue. See back cover for address.

What you really need to know about

Moving House with Feng Shui

Jane Purr

ESSENTIALS

Published in 2000 by
How To Books Ltd, 3 Newtec Place,
Magdalen Road, Oxford OX4 1RE, United Kingdom
Tel: (01865) 793806   Fax: (01865) 248780
email: info@howtobooks.co.uk
www.howtobooks.co.uk

British Library Cataloguing in Publication Data.
A catalogue record for this book is available from
the British Library.

Edited by Diana Brueton
Cover design by Shireen Nathoo Design
Cover copy by Sallyann Sheridan
Produced for How To Books by Deer Park Productions
Typeset by PDQ Typesetting, Newcastle-under-Lyme, Staffordshire
Printed and bound by Hillman Printers, Frome, Somerset

NOTE: The material contained in this book is set out in good faith for
general guidance and no liability can be accepted for loss or expense
incurred as a result of relying in particular circumstances on
statements made in the book. The laws and regulations are complex
and liable to change, and readers should check the current position
with the relevant authorities before making personal arrangements.

ESSENTIALS *is an imprint of*
How To Books

Contents

Preface

So you're in. The house is yours. And the garden and the garage. And the wallpaper and the bathroom tiles and the carpet and the front gate. It's all yours.

But where to begin? What should come first? Will you ever settle in at all? Of course you will and probably have done before, but for most of us moving house will always be an endurance test. It never gets any easier no matter how many times we do it.

This book can't remove the sheer hard grind and natural sense of disorientation associated with relocating, nor will it tell you how to unpack your goods or choose your furniture; these are personal decisions. What it *can* do is serve as a guide for **creating and managing the energy in your new home** – from day one.

This book is intended to complement *Sell Your Home Using Feng Shui* but works equally as a tool in its own right. It is also suitable for people wishing to implement basic feng shui even if they are already established in their home. The tips and suggestions are relevant to most environments and are not exclusively targeted at relocaters.

Moving House with Feng Shui is not meant to be an all-encompassing work on feng shui. There are plenty of academic references available for this purpose and if this short book inspires the reader to go on to investigate feng shui in greater depth, that will be a bonus. In the first instance, however, it simply aims to help people **settle into their new home quickly and easily using sound and established feng shui principles**. It offers suggestions about things you might like to take into account before making changes to your new home and about the order in which you tackle jobs. It looks at your place in your new community and how you can take that place promptly and with the minimum of fuss.

Most of all it encourages you to weave feng shui not only into your new home but into your new life.

Jane Purr

DEDICATION
To Katie and Eve

1 About Feng Shui

Feng shui is the study of nature and its effects on the health and wealth of mankind at any given time and place.

Things that really matter

1 **UNDERSTANDING WHAT FENG SHUI IS**

2 **UNDERSTANDING WHAT FENG SHUI IS NOT**

3 **KNOWING HOW TO USE FENG SHUI**

4 **UNDERSTANDING CHI**

5 **UNDERSTANDING YIN AND YANG**

Reams have been written about feng shui, but much of it is both complex and confusing. Feng shui is simply one branch of an ancient Eastern study based on the understanding of the existence of a **single vibrational energy** throughout the universe. Today, vibrational energy is recognised not only by Eastern practitioners of the energetic arts and sciences but also by many contemporary Western physicists.

This single vibrational energy is common to all things, both organic and inorganic. In the East it is known as *chi* – life's breath. The Chinese do not appear to have been the only ancient people to have had an understanding of chi. It seems that the Mayans, the American Indians and the Ancients of Europe, amongst others, were aware of this energy too.

According to feng shui thought, chi can be divided into **two opposed – although complementary and interlinked**

– energies: *yin* and *yang*. From here it separates further into the **five energetic essences**: fire, earth, metal, water, wood. All practices linked to the study of vibrational energy aim to **create and maintain a balance** of these elements. In acupuncture, for instance, the intention is to ensure a balance of energy throughout the body.

Feng shui is used to identify and correct areas of energy inappropriate to human habitation, and to enhance areas construed as more auspicious. In addition it is used to calculate compatibility between man and place. But the principle is always the same: **to protect and then to enhance**. Only then may we prosper.

① UNDERSTANDING WHAT FENG SHUI *IS*

Feng shui is an established Chinese scientific study of the cause and effect of cosmic and terrestrial vibrational energy. It is:

- an **art form** – in its creation of balance and harmony
- a **skill** – in its identification and implementation
- an **enabling tool**
- **common sense** – the obvious
- part of a much **wider understanding** of vibrational energy.

② UNDERSTANDING WHAT FENG SHUI *IS NOT*

Feng shui is not magic – it will not create overnight miracles. Nor is it a religion – it is simply a system which recommends living with the forces that exist within nature. Feng shui is not:

- a belief system – it is a fact not a faith
- a cure-all or crutch – it will benefit most those who want to help themselves in the first instance

- another New Age bandwagon – it has been in constant use for thousands of years
- a con – simply because something is out of one's sphere of knowledge and experience does not mean to say it does not exist and is not effective. Keep an open mind.

③ KNOWING HOW TO USE FENG SHUI

Feng shui should be used sparingly and with respect. Approach it defensively in the first instance – ensure health *then* aim for wealth. Use it with intent – *know* what you want from it – and with integrity, avoiding greed and maliciousness.

④ UNDERSTANDING CHI

Chi is reciprocal. It emanates health but it is also sustained and revived by healthy phenomena.

Chi on the move is carried in the air. It follows obvious easy routes: traditionally, streams and rivers. Today it will just as surely follow roads and motorways. It will skim corners and cubby holes as it winds its way along and may benefit or neglect living things depending whereabouts they are sited on the route. It will move faster along a straight route than a curve and will slow and meander when the path is undulating. Expanses of water, as opposed to *waterways*, encourage it to stay a while and create an ambient environment.

- Chi gets to the most inaccessible places in the end but by the time it gets there it is sluggish and lacking in vitality.
- Make the route too easy, however, and it will whoosh through without giving those along the way the benefit

of its health-giving properties.

The key is balance. Invite chi to your front door up a gently curved path and it will reach the house at an acceptable pace and benefit the garden along the way. You want it to reach your entrance neither too quickly (**yang**), nor too slowly (**yin**).

⑤ UNDERSTANDING YIN AND YANG

Yin and yang energies are complete opposites, yet complement and balance each other perfectly. Basically yin is dark, yang is light; yin is female, yang is male; yin is water, yang is fire and so on. Neither is right nor wrong, both are necessary. An imbalance of either may create inauspicious influences and an unhealthy environment. Much of the job of the feng shui practitioner is to **identify imbalances of energy and recommend measures to correct them**.

MAKING WHAT MATTERS WORK FOR YOU

✓ This is your opportunity to create a home and garden which emanate the kind of energy you want to live with.

✓ Whilst you might have been more than happy with your previous home there were probably parts of it that you always felt could have been improved – some imbalances which could have been rectified. This is your chance to learn from that and work the energy in this new house so that it better meets your needs.

✓ Enabling you to understand what creates a balanced environment is what this book is all about.

2 Moving In

Home is where the heart is. Your energy – your
chi – breathes life into it.
J. Purr

3

things that
really matter

1 **RE-ROOTING AND SETTLING IN**

2 **SORTING OUT SPACE**

3 **ROOM USAGE**

So you're in. And this is the house that you ... *what exactly?*
– yearned for, ended up with, compromised over?
Whatever, you're here.

And here's something to remember about feng shui and
homemaking: there are two possible ways to go about it.
(a) You choose the ideal feng shui location with your ideal
feng shui directions and have your house built accordingly
(lucky you).
or
(b) you make do with what you get and enlist the aid of
feng shui to help you make the best of it.

Most of us fall into the second category and there's
nothing wrong with that. Every house has *something*
appealing about it, some fortunate aspect. Even if you're
there under duress you'll be able to find some nook or
cranny, some view, some eccentricity about the place that
excites your imagination – if you let it. **Home is what we**

choose to make it. It can be hell or it can be a sanctuary. To a certain extent, the choice is yours. Without you and your input it's simply bricks and mortar, plaster and lathe.

Success is getting what you want. Happiness is liking what you get.

 RE-ROOTING AND SETTLING IN

Despite the fact that you may have parted properly from your last house and paid your respects to the home you left behind, relocating is still a wrench.

This is because the division between you and your home can become almost indistinguishable. In the first stages you mould your home; after that your home moulds you. You become as one, inseparable. It's therefore quite natural that no matter how sensible the reasoning behind this move, nor how much you can justify relocating into this new house, you still feel a sense of loss.

You will probably feel disorientated too, out on a limb with nowhere to turn. What you are going through is **a period of adjustment**. You are at the in-between stage. Although you have a house, you do not yet have a home. Don't force it. This reaction is absolutely natural. However, the following steps may help you find your feet more easily.

- Begin as you mean to go on by **calling the house home** and encourage the rest of the family to do the same.
- Wander round your new home by yourself. Stop in each room and feel your way around. Pick at the wallpaper, lift the corner of the carpet, poke at the paint work, trace the woodwork with your fingers, breathe on the windows. It's called **marking your territory**. Most animals do it. Most humans usually do it without even

thinking about it, but sometimes we forget to allow ourselves time for such rituals.

- On moving day, try to **create at least one pleasant area** as soon as you put a foot through the door of your new house. Whilst others are ensuring that boxes and crates are going into the right rooms, you set up a home-from-home. Open that box you specially prepared with tea/coffee, fruitcake, kettle, linen etc. Pick something out of your new garden, even if it's only a dandelion, and stick it in a jug. Turn a tea chest upside-down, throw a cloth over the top and lay out your feast.

- Place the flowers in the middle and call everyone in for refreshments. They'll laugh, think you're mad, but they will also enjoy the sentiment even if only secretly, and **raise a toast to your new home**. You will have broken the ice – and bread – for the first time under your new roof.

② SORTING OUT SPACE

Before you begin unpacking anything think about some traditional feng shui pointers with regard to room allocation.

Room allocation will probably have been done, to some extent, before you moved in. Your criteria for this will no doubt have been based on your individual needs and the constraints of the house design.

In terms of Form School feng shui it is considered preferential to site what are known as **foul energy areas** (bathroom, toilet, kitchen, utility) towards the rear of the house. Traditionally these would have been located behind the house and well away from the building. For the sake of convenience, however, most Western homes have included these areas inside the house itself. If you have any option in the matter, therefore, or are considering a new kitchen, bathroom etc, do think about siting all plumbing outlets as close as possible to the external rear wall. **Wash your pollution straight out of the house** instead of detouring it under the floorboards.

Are your kitchen sink and toilet sited to the front of the house? Is your toilet next to the entrance location? If so, keep the seat down and the door shut. Consider changing its use to a closet. Future investment might allow you to shift the kitchen sink to a side wall as opposed to the front, but be prepared for external plumbing costs. In the short term, ensure the area has a solid door and keep it closed. Surround and disguise the stench pipe/drain at the front of the house with plenty of lively foliage. Keep it healthy and keep yourself healthy at the same time.

Do not even consider turning the under-stairs cupboard into a macerating toilet. Sorry, but staircases are often located in the centre – the heart – of the home. *Not* an area in which to be churning up sewage. This place should be kept clean, clear and unblocked in every respect.

Also think seriously before hacking well-proportioned bedrooms into miniature sleeping areas with ensuite bathrooms. This generally changes the original rectangular shape of the room into an L-shaped space and it loses its balance. If you must do this (and there's no doubt adjoining bathrooms can be very convenient), bear in mind the following Form School guidelines:

- Site **door to bathroom** next to door to bedroom, not facing into the bedroom proper.
- Have **toilet/sink/bath/shower outlet** on outside wall or as near to as possible. Do not allow **waste** to drain away under floor or around walls.
- Attempt not to position **bedheads** against walls with

toilets backing onto the other side of them.

- **Toilets** should not be visible from the door. If the position cannot be moved, think about building a half-wall or screen of some sort to shield the view.
- Try to make sure the room has a **window** or ceiling velux.
- Ensure an **extraction fan** is installed.
- Keep **toilet seat** down and door to bathroom closed at all times.
- Ensure there is a good 15 cm growth room above the head of the tallest person using any **mirrors** in the bathroom. You should be able to stand tall and still see room for potential over your head.
- Recreate a symmetrical shape to the **sleeping area** by making an anteroom out of the space between the bedroom door and the end of the short leg of the L. Hang a clear beaded curtain across the entry space, or consider some narrow glass double doors. Use a material which allows light through, you do not want to create a dark passage.

③ ROOM USAGE

Consider how each room, each section of the house can be put to best use.

- The most yin, most **supported area** of the house should be the back. Here (the notional Northern area of the house, symbolically known as the Black Turtle) it should be quiet and still. An ideal area for bedrooms, away from traffic and the general activity of front-of-house rooms.
- Studys are best located in a **quieter area** of the home also. An obvious fact perhaps, but one easily overlooked

in the rush to allocate people to places.

- Vice versa, place rooms requiring **light and yang energy** towards the front of the house – living rooms, games rooms and so on.

- Small, dark **unattractive areas** can be put to use as utility rooms and storage cupboards, or perhaps as a separate toilet.

- The **centre of the house** should really be used by all the household as a representation of health, wealth and general prosperity. A hall table with fresh flowers and a picture depicting family unity can be particularly uplifting. Do not use this area for storage as this tends to encourage stagnation – the last thing you want here.

MAKING WHAT MATTERS WORK FOR YOU

✓ Remember as you gaze around your new but piecemeal living room, wistfully recalling the wonderful one you left behind, that the shifting out, moving on and moving in process is both exciting *and* unnerving.

✓ *Expect* to feel a complexity of emotions during this time, and these emotions to be fleeting and vivid. You may be on a 'high' one minute and the next, laid low with the enormity of it all. Everyone feels the same when they move house.

✓ Keep occupied. Actually you have no choice but to be during this process. It will distract you from the day-to-day-doubts and insecurities that are assailing you.

✓ Don't forget it was *you* who created that wonderful living room you left behind. Have some confidence in yourself. You are quite capable of doing it again, only this time you have the opportunity to do something different!

3 The Castle Walls

Change brings life.
(English proverb)

3

things that
really matter

1 **THE ARMCHAIR CONFIGURATION**

2 **APPLYING FORM SCHOOL TODAY**

3 **KNOWING HOW IT AFFECTS YOU**

The first step towards implementing any system of feng shui is to ensure that the premises are **defended from unhealthy influences**, also that the property is secure and that any inauspicious energies are reduced or negated. This means taking into account, amongst other things, the stability, structure and direction of the building. Once this aspect of feng shui has been properly addressed then the occupants may indulge in the luxury of **enhancing their home and playing up good energies**.

This section, then, deals with the more pragmatic (although to some, perhaps, less interesting) aspect of **protecting and stabilising the home**.

 THE ARMCHAIR CONFIGURATION

The ancient feng shui masters would have spent days **chasing the dragon**, ie walking the land looking for the healthiest site in terms of **sheng chi** (good energy) on which to build a dwelling. This was and is known as **Form School** feng shui. Literally, it took into account the forms of the land, the terrain around the site, before the decision was made to actually begin construction. When they finally found the ideal spot it would have to conform to the following rules:

- The **back** of the site would have:
  - faced magnetic compass direction **North**
  - been supported by mountains or trees
  - been known as the **Black Turtle** area.
- The **front** of the site would have:
  - faced magnetic compass direction **South**
  - looked across slightly declining pasture land
  - been known as the **Red Phoenix** area.
- The **right** of the site would have:
  - faced magnetic compass direction **West**
  - enclosed this side of the property with lower hills
  - been known as the **White Tiger** area.
- The **left** of the site would have:
  - faced magnetic compass direction **East**
  - enclosed the side of the property with trees
  - been known as the **Green Dragon** area.

The dwelling itself would have been built onto an area of relatively flat land in the centre of this ideal space and if the inhabitants were very fortunate, would have had running water meandering across the South of the site in a 'hugging' gesture (see Figure 1). Today this ideal layout is sometimes known as the **armchair configuration**; high back, lower arms, open view to the front. You are sited comfortably in the middle.

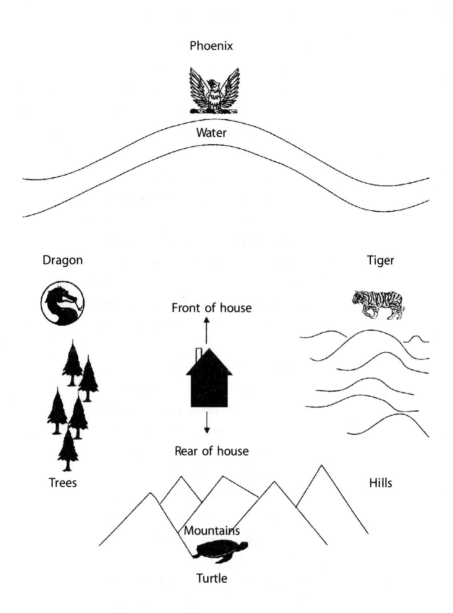

Figure 1. Ideal Form School Location.

APPLYING FORM SCHOOL TODAY

How do we interpret these ground rules today? Slightly differently in fact. Today the directions North, South, West and East are often no longer magnetic compass directions, but *notional* directions. Understanding contemporary Form School now becomes easier if we actually stop referring to North, South, West and East altogether and use instead the terms Turtle, Phoenix, Tiger and Dragon. Many houses built today do not conform to the original Form School ideal and may have their front doors facing in any direction. Sometimes the house faces South, sometimes it does not. This does not make it 'wrong'. What is important is that the principles of support and protection are adhered to:

- **Back of the building: Turtle**. A building should be protected to the rear by hills or dense trees. These days we may interpret this as a high, solid wall or fence or perhaps another building. The original intention was that nothing should be able to get between the house and its metaphorical ramparts. This line of defence gave the occupants physical protection and therefore peace of mind. They could rest easy, secure in the knowledge that their backs were not exposed to any sort of danger be it from the weather or the 'enemy'!

- **Front of the building: Phoenix**. A building should have a clear view to the front of the property. It should not be overshadowed by anything immediately in front of it and the building should be slightly raised to avoid the risk of flood. A front garden or shared common land acts in this way today, allowing us to see what is coming towards the house and also providing a healthy sweep of land for chi to wash over before it enters the building. This is crucial as the entrance location is the most important area of any dwelling.

- **Right side of the building: Tiger**. A building should be enclosed to this side by hills or mountains, somewhat lower than those supporting the rear of the site. They should not be so high as to entirely block out the sun from this direction. These hills would have protected the building from the elements but also to some extent from predators. Today we may interpret the Tiger as a neighbouring building if there are no hills to speak of. Cultivating the neighbours will do no harm either as they can act as protectors (as you can for them), looking out for your home when you are away.
- **Left side of the building: Dragon**. A building ought to be supported to this side by greenery, trees, hills or moors. This area is particularly important in feng shui as it represents the prosperity of those within the building. Again the total height should not be so tall as to block light. The Dragon should also act as a defensive barrier in a similar way to the Tiger.

 KNOWING HOW IT AFFECTS YOU

Where does your home fit into all this? You want your lives to be as auspicious as possible in this new location. You want to feel at ease, prosperous, creative and expansive as soon as you can in this house. If this is truly the case then begin by putting Form School feng shui into action now.

Start with the **Turtle** area of your home. Take a look out of your back door, or one of your back windows if the back door doesn't actually open out to the rear of the property. What do you see – garden and then a wall, perhaps? Is the wall or fence solid, secure, stable – is it high enough? Would it be difficult to climb? Does it act as a competent

wind break? Would it shield the house in bad weather?
Would it deter undesirables?

If you have answered no to any of the questions, maybe
you should consider setting this situation straight before you
even begin thinking about paint and paper for that new
front room you were planning. While internal decor is
undoubtedly important in feng shui, it is not *as* important
as the external defence of your property.

Consider the following points to help you establish a
sound Turtle behind your home.

- Double up on **protection and support** by introducing
  trees or shrubs along the inside of your back garden wall
  in this area.
- Greenery also encourages wildlife and both bring
  living, healthy energy to your garden and home.
- Look carefully at what you are planting however, and
  ensure that your choice in garden design is not only
  right for you, but for your immediate neighbours. It
  should also be **appropriate to the neighbourhood**
  generally. Leylandii for instance, no doubt appropriate in
  the right circumstances, has been abused by many
  people and turned into a horticultural weapon. This is
  not in the spirit of feng shui.
- Ultimately what matters is that the back of the house is
  supported and not exposed, eg you would not find an
  open field or rushing river behind the house.

The reasoning behind all this is to enable the occupants
of the building, your family, to sleep soundly in their beds
knowing that the house is secure to the rear. Secure in this
instance meaning protected from the elements and
intruders.

Moving on to the **Phoenix** area of your property, what

do you see facing the front of your home? Garden – or scrub? A paved area and then road? A statue or bus stop, perhaps? A car right outside the front door? None of these aspects is particularly auspicious, except the garden and even then it should be well maintained. Neglected lawns and beds are poor feng shui. Pavement is not bad but can be improved with pots and containers (filled with colour and foliage of course). A statue or some other 'blocking' object will also affect the home in a negative way.

Measures can be taken to improve the situation, as follows:

- Start at the **curb** and move forward towards the house. Assess the situation. Is the gate sound, in need of paint or oil – is it there at all in fact or is it missing? What about the front hedge/fence/wall? What sort of condition is that in? Replace, upgrade and recondition as necessary.

- Walk up the **garden path** and consider its state. Is the lawn healthy; do the containers need filling; are the shrubs thriving – *are* there any shrubs for that matter, or flowers? If the answers are negative, get to work and set the situation right.

- Now stand on the **front doorstep** and look into the street. Is the view blocked in any way? Is the step itself a mess, piled high with old shoes and dead plant life? If so clear them and move anything else that stops chi from entering your entrance location. Also wash the step, paint the door, polish the brass, fix the doorbell, plant some flowers – *and attract some chi.*

- Check the condition of the **front of house** paintwork and brickwork and clean the windows. You've loads of work to do and windows are at the bottom of the list, but chi enters through the eyes (windows) of the house and dirt inhibits their vision. Clean them and let the energy flow in, even if there is other work in progress. Get the window-cleaner in more regularly if this is the case and notice how good the house feels.

Just because your house is under construction doesn't mean everything else has to come to a standstill. Keep on top of the mess – don't let it build up or try to save it up for a huge purge. Dust and clutter grind you down on a daily basis. Try to tidy and clean each day rather than attempt to live in a filthy state in the hope that you will be able to have a grand clean-up at the end of it. Don't get into that 'it's not worth it' frame of mind. Cleaning up muck from your home is *always* worth it.

Waiting for the 'end' when builders are involved can take forever: in the meantime you're collapsing under the strain of living in a building site. Keep on top of it and keep the energy flowing.

Consider the **Tiger** side of your home by standing in your back garden, facing the back of your house and looking to the right. Hills here would be great, or perhaps some mature trees. Another house of about the same height as your own is also good. A vista of flat open land is not so supportive and can be rectified with the erection of a sound fence or wall, or a line of trees.

Taking the same position in the back garden and looking to the left will reveal the shape of the **Dragon** area of your location. Again, hills or trees would be ideal to provide the protection you need to this side of your home. The dragon is most important in terms of the financial stability of the household. If you have no dragon, create one. A generous evergreen hedge would serve the purpose (but bear in mind previous guidelines about Leylandii).

To summarise, in dealing with the four animal directions of your new home you will begin to understand more about how your house stands in its location. This will help you get to know your property more intimately. Taking the opportunity to look closely while you still have the objective vision of a newcomer enables you to see both the strengths and weaknesses in the property. Go on to enhance the strengths and correct the weaknesses and make this new house work for you.

It takes dedication to create a home, time to allow yourself to grow into a new environment. Nestbuilding is more than just a natural urge; it's a labour of love, a longterm manifestation of positive energy.

People make a home. Interior design can do a lot; the right location is undoubtedly helpful but in the end it needs human commitment to produce a happy household. Feng Shui can help in this process but it is not a quick fix. It is more of an enabling exercise. It shows you a different way of looking at things. An alternative view of life.

MAKING WHAT MATTERS WORK FOR YOU

✓ You're in, you're unpacked (mostly), you've come to terms with what you've left behind and you're making the most of what is to come. Good, but pace yourself.

✓ This process can be very tiring. You are likely to be on edge, honed and very aware – simply because you are in an unknown environment. Your senses will be on guard to protect you from unforeseen problems. This is instinctive and should ease off as you become more comfortable in your new surroundings.

✓ Use the moment to gather information that you would normally not be so conscious of. You will soon lose this heightened conscious awareness. After a while in this new house it will not be as easy for you to *experience* with the clarity you have at the moment. Go through all the pointers above while your antennae are still finely attuned.

✓ Once your data has been collected and you know what needs to be done to secure your home, set the process in motion. Then you can begin to relax and settle in.

4 Looking at the Inside

If houses are people, a home is a friend.
J. Purr

4 things that really matter

1 **ENERGISING YOUR UTILITIES**

2 **USING LIGHT AND COLOUR**

3 **SHAPE AND PROPORTION**

4 **APPLYING TEXTURE AND PATTERN**

Now that protective measures have been assessed and any work needed is under way, you can begin looking at the **internal layout and decor** of your new home. Some people find this the most interesting aspect of creating a home; others prefer to be involved in the initial planning and design and the actual construction.

In feng shui **both aspects are important**. Each is relevant in the production of a healthy, positive, prosperous living environment. Each should be given equal consideration. However, the order in which these aspects are taken into account is crucial.

The structure of the house represents the skin of the living organism (the home) inside. It should be stable, secure and weatherproof. Without these considerations, internal well-being is in jeopardy. Once the extremities are protected using the principle of the four animals (see Chapter 3) the **function of the inside** may be taken into consideration.

① ENERGISING YOUR UTILITIES

In many ways we live in no more than glorified caves.

Comfortably protected from the elements in our convenient and cosy homes, the downside of this rarefied existence is that our senses have become dulled. Compared to our ancestors most of us infrequently feel the sun on our face, the wind in our hair, the grass under our bare feet. Survival in those days, in an often brutal outside environment, necessarily sharpened our senses producing a synerginetic effect known as intuition – our *sixth sense* if you like.

Much of feng shui is about bringing nature inside.

The brain – both consciously and unconsciously – reacts to symbolic manifestations of all things natural. They activate our senses as if we were experiencing them in the flesh and keep our reactions toned up. Nature keeps us sharp and fresh, prevents stagnation and poor health. Hence the importance of giving serious consideration to everything with which you surround yourself.

In this, your new home, you have the opportunity to **reconsider the way you are experiencing life**. Why not try to establish a better quality reproduction of nature? Think about the following:

- Your **water**. How pure is it? Even some bottled water contains minerals which we could really do without. Fit a purifier or filter under the sink.
- Your **air**. Closing off chilly draughts around the house also means barring fresh air. The internal air can then become positively ionised which may in turn lead to a stale and unhealthy atmosphere around the house. Ionisers both clean the air and negatively charge it so it becomes similar to the type of invigorating air you

might experience at the seaside. Look at industrial or hospital-strength ionisers for best efficiency. Likewise your vacuum cleaner; use something which isn't simply going to redistribute the dust and dirt around the house.

- Your **lighting**. Sunlight experienced through generous and sparklingly clean windows is best of course, but failing that look at the range of *daylight bulbs* on the market. These replicate the sun when it's at its zenith on a cloud-free day. Exposed to the full spectrum of colours we receive from such light we not only *see* better but *feel* better too as it helps to stave off SAD syndrome, a problem for anyone living in a drizzly environment. These bulbs can be expensive however so use them selectively: in the kitchen, over the home desk, as a reading light. Nowadays they are even available as fluorescent tubes.

- Your **heating**. We all know about the various energy saving measures on the market, which are getting better all the time, but don't rule out the idea of real flame alongside your central heating. Contained stoves are worth considering too. Not only are they amazingly efficient, but they bring heart to the home. Every home should have some sort of hearth with a real flame even if it's only a huge candle placed on a shelf acting as a mantle.

② USING LIGHT AND COLOUR

Light works alongside colour as a feng shui balancing aid in the home.

The majority of houses are sold on the buyer's **perception of light** in a house. The more light, the better – but it should be light without glare. Harsh, direct light can be too yang but can easily be dissipated with the strategic use of lace or voile. It's nice to have the option of muting a room that has too much light. Generally, most rooms in the Northern hemisphere do not have enough light to mute and what is available is often cold and patchy.

North-facing rooms tend to have light that is **cool and fairly unchanging** (yin). You can rely on the light you find in these rooms to stay pretty much the same from day to day, season to season. But that's about all it has going for it. It's not flattering, rather, it's unforgiving light. Artists like it; the rest of us tend to congregate in South-facing rooms where we'll find the warmth and cheer (yang) we seek.

Colour can enhance light. Light can enhance colour. The whole subject is a study in itself and the addition of **artificial lighting** creates a further dimension. It is worth giving some consideration to a few ground rules however.

- As a *guideline* only:

  Yang colours are: red, orange, yellow.

  Yin colours are: violet, blue, green.

- Add white to any colour and it becomes a **tint** (lighter and airier – more yang). Add black and it becomes a **shade** (darker and moodier – more yin). Add red and it becomes warmer; add blue and it becomes cooler.

- Work out which **direction your house faces**. The light coming in through the window will affect the colours in that room, eg brown in a North room with cold light can look mink or taupe. Brown in a South-facing room may look salmon or terracotta.

- If you are not sure **how a paint colour will look** in a particular room, tear off the end of a shoe box and paint the inside with your chosen colour, creating a dolls house room. Leave it on a table in the room you want to paint and watch how the colour changes during the day as the sun moves round. Also notice how it alters at night when you put your indoor lights on. If you have any fabric samples for curtains or covers, pin a cutting inside and see how it changes with the light.

Having a trial run helps avoid big decorating mistakes. Blue is a lovely colour but is it really suitable for a North-facing bathroom? Not unless you want to shiver your way through your morning shower – far too yin! Yet warm, cornflower blue in a sunny front room can work very well. You're aiming for a balance in the home and creating balance is a skill. Spend some time developing it.

③ SHAPE AND PROPORTION

As important as colour and light are shape and proportion.

Consider the following when planning furniture and its positioning in your new home:

- **Curves and sweeping lines** are good for people and (yin) nurturing energy. They allow ease of movement and the gentle eddying of chi. They are good for bedrooms and areas used for relaxation.
- **Angles** promote activity, action, innovation. Good for offices, dining rooms, creative settings and areas where you want to stay awake.
- Sweep an eye around the **walls** of your rooms. Is all the furniture tall, open and contemporary in design (yang)? Or is it squat, dark wood and antique (yin)? Think about mixing the heights so you have a variation in silhouette. Don't allow your eye to be pulled downward too much. Pictures should be placed with the centre at eye level.
- Mix **new with old**. Balance the energies.

- Try to avoid placing large **dark objects** against window walls.
- Watch what you place on the **top of units**. Cumbersome ornaments and large books can look unwieldy and feel as if something's looming over you.
- Don't **overwhelm a small room** with heavy drapes unless you are going over the top with ceiling to floor, wall–to-wall curtains.
- Large paintings in a small room might make an **interesting juxtaposition** but avoid doing the same with large furniture, it simply looks bulky. Rooms should invite you in, not present an obstacle course when you open the door. If they discourage you, they will do the same to chi.

④ APPLYING TEXTURE AND PATTERN

Texture has a more subtle effect on us than colour or light but it is equally as important.

Too many hard, flat, reflective surfaces can make us jumpy, hyperactive, feel exposed and vulnerable. It looks stylish, which is why many contemporary offices are designed in this way, but it feels uncomfortable and puts us on edge. In fact it's far too *yang*.

Conversely, the typically overstuffed, draped and swathed Victorian parlour, hung with lace, tapestry, chenille and fringing has a suffocating, stultifying effect on us today. It brings everything to a standstill. This excess of *yin* energy can lead to misery and lethargy. Avoid the above scenarios in your home by:

- combining a balance of hard or reflective surfaces (glass, metal, polished wood, ceramic) with soft or matte finishes (fabric, leather, wicker, terracotta)

- using pattern, another useful tool for the feng shui decorator. It can break up large, intimidating spaces or crowd in on you until you feel surrounded. An overabundance of florals can have a very busy effect so choose and use your patterns with care.

To encapsulate: if you want an area to be slightly more relaxing, incorporate a *little* more soft texture with some yin colours. On the other hand, if you want to encourage conversation and liveliness, veer towards yang hues and a few well-placed glass or metal objects.

MAKING WHAT MATTERS WORK FOR YOU

✓ Use this opportunity to incorporate feng shui into the very structure of your home by improving the quality of the elements around you. Filter your water, cleanse your air, brighten your lighting and feel the difference a domestic de-tox makes.

✓ Continue on this healthful energy theme by creating balance for the senses in your use of colour, texture, shape and proportion. Weigh carefully every aspect of your decor and allow your ideas to come to fruition.

✓ Resist rushing in just to make your mark. Clean and tidy is enough for now. Take your time, let the house speak to you.

✓ Remember: houses are built, homes evolve.

5 Ensuring a Flow

He that follows nature is never out of his way.
(English proverb)

4

things that really matter

1 **CREATING BALANCE AND HARMONY**

2 **KNOWING THE IMPORTANCE OF SYMBOLS**

3 **USING SPACE AND OBJECTS**

4 **MOVEMENT AND STILLNESS**

There is a saying in feng shui: **everything around you calls to you**. In fact everything in your home is *telling you a story, demanding your attention*. It therefore makes sense to ensure that all your worldy goods are not only telling you a good story but also that you're not being distracted by too many conflicting stories at once.

You're aiming for harmony, an environment where everything flows seamlessly together, where everything conspires to make you feel safe, relaxed and in control and feng shui is *felt*, not announced by trinkets and dingle-dangles. This is feng shui inherent in the home. It has become an intrinsic part of the make-up of the house and the people in it. Each supports the other. The energy flows, they are balanced.

 CREATING BALANCE AND HARMONY

This process of **integrated feng shui** is not a static one. Maintaining it requires constant vigilance and flexibility.

The decor of a house designed for summer may well suit its purpose. The home provides a cool, refreshing, airy environment for the householders. The feng shui is good, it provides a contrast to the heat and glare outside. Come winter, this internal environment is inappropriate. It is now chilly, still and uninviting. Things must change. Bring in the throws, fur rugs, soft cushions, paisley drapes. Turn up the heat, light the fire. Once again you have created balance and are meeting the criteria for good feng shui.

Simplistic? To an extent. In this instance the reference was to a single change, a seasonal change, but *everything* changes all the time. Wake up in a depressed mood and what do you do? Snuggle up if you can, put on a cosy old sweater, head for the chocolate, perhaps turn on the telly or go for a run. You try to compensate by making yourself feel good. **You are balancing yourself instinctively all the time**.

Your home needs the same treatment, the same respect. We may not be able to afford to redecorate each spring, but we can put some daffodils in a vase, stow away the heavy throws, change the dark bed cover for a lightweight lace one and so on. This balancing process applies to all things, even the food on our plate. Nasty, cold, wet day (yin)? Let's have some steaming homemade soup (yang). Sweltering outside (yang) – what about a salad (yin)? You can apply the concept to everything.

A balanced house is a harmonious home.

Don't let your house get stale. Use every opportunity for incorporating change into your surrounding environment. It will keep you on your toes. But don't regard it as an onerous task. It should really be second nature to you, something you do naturally as a matter of course. **Creating**

balance is about maintaining health, and looking after your health is a basic survival instinct. Somewhere along the way we have forgotten, that's all.

 KNOWING THE IMPORTANCE OF SYMBOLS

Another feng shui saying, **everything you see around you comes out in your behaviour**, sums up the importance of the symbols you surround yourself with. You can take this saying one step further to really get an understanding of this aspect of feng shui by enlarging it as follows: *everything you experience around you has an effect on your attitude and behaviour.*

Symbols can set off deep, primitive reactions in human beings. Sometimes these can be positive, at other times negative. On a subconscious as well as conscious level we are absorbing all that is going on around us all the time. Children are particularly receptive in this respect but none of us is immune.

Surround yourself with darkness, heaviness, stillness (too much yin) and you will probably find yourself becoming miserable. Conversely, hyperactivity will be the result of too much bright colour, loud music, harsh light and extreme flavour (overly yang). Look at your current surroundings; even if they are temporary they will still be having an effect on you on a day-to-day basis. Consider the following:

- **Paintings/prints**: do they depict positive, uplifting scenes or they are unhappy, violent or lonely?
- **Photographs**: do they bring a good memory to mind or would you rather not be reminded of that particular time, place, person?
- **Books**: are they worth a re-read or are you simply hanging on to them to bulk out your library?

- **Ornaments**: do you really like them or are they simply there because they were wedding/birthday gifts and you haven't the nerve to put them away?
- **Souvenirs**: can you honestly say they enhance your life or have they just become a habit?
- **Furniture**: is it useful, stable, attractive and comfortable or impractical, flimsy, ugly and awkward?
- **Colour**: does it soothe, calm or uplift you or does it unsettle, provoke or depress you?

Are your answers mostly on the negative side? If so perhaps you should use this opportunity to make a new beginning in terms of what you allow to have an influence over you.

A word here about **kitsch** in the home. Everything has its place and the home is not it for this type of decor. Kitsch is usually favoured by young people with fast-moving lives. They are more often out of their homes than in and, thankfully, are not influenced to any great extent by the detritus around them. While a single piece of kitsch per room can be construed as witty, a welcome twist of the surreal in an otherwise entirely harmonious setting, a whole room or – horrors – a whole house, is simply a bore.

To grasp that something is meant to be kitsch you have to get the 'joke'. Often owners of kitsch homes find it necessary to explain the 'point' of their choice of decor to visitors who simply find it bemusing or intimidating. Like a failed joke it then loses its impact and becomes a little embarrassing. The person who doesn't 'get it' feels intimidated and uncomfortable.

Kitsch is a form of inverted snobbery. It suggests that those who find themselves unamused by it have no sense of humour or are incapable of appreciating irony. But irony as a decorative form is hard to live with. It quickly wears thin revealing in all its banality the dubious taste beneath. Be wary of it. Irony is saying somethng you don't mean. To surround yourself with ironic decor is of necesssity to be constantly reminding yourself that the grotesque is amusing. Images of kitsch, if not consciously sugared with humour, have a souring effect on the subconscious. This is a very tiring way to live. Your home as one long joke. Day in day out. Constantly looking for a new audience to show it off to.

This form of ostentation has no place in feng shui so try to avoid it. Apart from anything else, living constantly amongst fluorescent colour, cheap materials and superficial images is undermining and unhealthy.

Feng shui is discreet and subtle, cheerful and joyous, calm and reflective, it never seeks to belittle or overwhelm.

USING SPACE AND OBJECTS

Furniture placement is what many people think about when feng shui comes to mind but equally important is **the space between the furniture**.

This new house is a chance for you to think through this aspect of **Form School** feng shui and create a home which allows for comfort, freedom of movement and a conducive flow of chi.

Rule of thumb: if you can move through a room with ease and can settle into it with a feeling of security, you have probably created a room that has good feng shui.

Consider the following:

- Do your **doors open to the wall**? If not, consider rehanging them (apart from the bedroom where they provide extra privacy). The extra space and light this gives a room is staggering. Don't forget you will probably need to have your light switches shifted too.

- While you're at it, why not have the **switch lowered** to wrist height? Ergonomically, it's much more appropriate and many new houses are being designed in this way. This is your chance – while the house is still evolving into the home you want.
- Does anything block your immediate **entrance to the room**? Do you have to wend your way around cumbersome bookcases? Remember chi will have the same trouble.
- Size your furniture **in proportion** to the size of the room, eg small chairs for small spaces, generous chairs for big, open spaces.
- Keep large, **heavy furniture** away from window walls.
- Keep alcoves and corners from becoming **stagnant areas** by bringing life to them. Use plants, light, water.
- Ensure you can get **beneath and behind** furniture. If you can get there to clean, chi can get there to energise.
- Don't position all furniture **around the walls** like a doctor's surgery. Move some of it forward and/or stand it at an angle.
- **Mix materials**. Mix light and shade. Use a little white, but also a little black. Try plains and patterns, matt and reflective surfaces.
- Leave some **space**. There's no need to cover every surface with ornaments, every chair with cushions, every shelf with books. Live with the *nothingness* for a while and see how you manage.

Chi should be encouraged to *meander* round an area, not rush through like a raging torrent. It should be invited to pause and collect itself for a while before moving on.

Chi which has overstayed its welcome becomes exhausted and depleted. It becomes worse than useless inasmuch as it becomes unhealthy, which brings us nicely on to the next section.

 MOVEMENT AND STILLNESS

At this point of the settling-in process you probably haven't yet worked out which areas of the house, or of each room, are going to become places of bustle and action and which will naturally turn themselves into cosy corners for peaceful moments.

- **Yang areas**, those places where things always seem to be going on, usually involve more than one person. Interaction seems to promote this expression of expansive energy.

- **Yin sites**, on the other hand, are often although not always places of solitude. The reading corner generally just comprises one person tucking into a good book but a religious building, for instance, can involve a mass of people. Given that this book is aimed at the domestic environment, however, it can probably be assumed that people as *individuals* in the home simply want a yin place for some peace and quiet and a chance to get away from everyone else.

- **Movement** can induce calm or activity depending on the context in which it is used. Picture a gently tumbling water feature in an open back garden. Despite the ambient noise of playing children, lawnmowers and barking dogs, the fountain will provide a distraction and focus the mind of anyone in its vicinity. What it offers is yin respite in an abundance of obvious yang activity.

- **Stillness** can make the same contribution. Heavy, deep,

dark and quiet objects fulfil this criterion. Think of a
mountain, still water, the cool glade – hardly party
material, more places for reflection, meditation, simply
for being quiet. Recreate this atmosphere with solid
objects of metal or stone, eg a garden rockery. Provide
sumptuous seating and low lamp lighting. Hang
pictures of people in repose, drowsing over a book in
the garden or enjoying a quiet drink. But do remember,
it's solitude you're looking for here, not loneliness, so
avoid anything with connotations of sadness.

Conversely, 'dead areas', or those places in the home
lacking oomph will be enlivened by the addition of
movement. Areas of this type usually include nooks and
crannies, understairs areas, alcoves, separate dining rooms,
guest rooms and rooms closed off seasonally.

Add movement to these parts of the home with music,
plants (upward and outward growing), the colours lacquer
red and imperial yellow, clocks with pendulums, mobiles
and chimes (not metal), crystals, fire and light. Leave doors
open, heat the areas occasionally, open windows, switch on
fans. Use paintings depicting activity – kites flying, boats
under sail, children playing, people dancing. Dogs are
good for yang movement. Cats for yin. Both bring their
own dynamic to the home.

*Most homes tend to evolve a balance of both stillness and movement
to suit their owner's needs.*

Sometimes a house can become too quiet or too frenetic
and that's when reassessment is called for. If people have
to leave the home to get some peace or look for a 'lift', you
know there's something amiss. Avoid this happening in
your home by making **both movement and stillness** an
integral part of your plans for the future.

MAKING WHAT MATTERS WORK FOR YOU

✓ Recognising that everything, ourselves included, is in a constant state of flux, moving and shifting from yin to yang and back again will enable you to implement changes in your environment as a matter of course. You will simply *feel* when things need to alter.

✓ Tweaking a home and adjusting yourself to meet your changing needs is healthy and prevents stagnation. This does not mean that change is required every minute of every day. Do not imagine you have to bring about change for change's sake. It will come quickly enough of its own accord.

✓ Balancing your environment both in terms of its physical layout and its subconscious symbolism maintains harmony in your life.

✓ Bringing all of the above to bear provides a support for your own personal chi.

6 Including the Outside

Happiness grows at our own fireside, and is not to be picked in strangers' gardens. D. Jerrold

3

things that
really matter

1 **ENHANCING THE FRONT FIRST**

2 **CHANGE OR MAINTAIN?**

3 **GOING FOR COLOUR OR GREEN?**

Feng shui doesn't stop at the front door. **It applies to your whole property** – your whole street and town – and more! But you can begin spreading the good word by applying it to your own property in the first instance – garden, garage and house. Who knows where it might take you? What you create around you should be so **attractive and vitalising** that you find others approaching you for your secret. Tell them about feng shui if they ask but don't foist it on them. Nothing is more off-putting than evangelization. If others want to know they will ask.

 ENHANCING THE FRONT FIRST

The front of the house and/or garden is the area which should be the first to indicate your interest in feng shui. You can create the most perfect interior by feng shui standards, but if the exterior is neglected it will negate much of the work you have done inside. The approach to your home and entrance location cannot be overemphasised in terms of its energetic importance. But this area is not just an enhancement to your own life; it should also **blend in with, and raise the quality of, the area in which your home is located**.

We all want to express our individuality and many people like to extend this creativity to the land around their home too. This is quite natural and the way in which this individuality manifests itself is what makes our streets and towns so interesting. A uniform approach to aesthetics soon becomes boring and dulls the senses. Other people's ideas can be stimulating and inspiring – how many of us can resist looking into a lighted window at night? We are curious about the different ways in which other people live their lives. However:

- The desire for individuality needs to be tempered when it comes to the outside of the home if the building is not to become jarring or an eyesore.
- An eyesore is not necessarily something ugly or tasteless in itself. It is often something which *just doesn't fit*.

While thankfully not commonplace, we have all seen houses which fall into this category. Unfortunately their owners seem to suffer from a narrowness of perception. It's as if their home exists in isolation from those around it; as if they are an island alone from their neighbours. While these houses provide amusement to the occasional passer-by, the tolerance of those living in the immediate vicinity is often desperately tried. Live and let live is pushed to the limit. However, none of us really want to legislate against personal expression. Instead we hope and to a certain extent expect, our neighbours will have the courtesy not to inflict their individuality on us too blatantly.

A property like this will generally be hard to sell. Few

people want to buy a house with too much 'character', nor do they want to live next to one. For this reason eyesore houses tend to undermine the retail value of properties in close proximity to them. Unfortunately the ensuing resentment does nothing to enhance community spirit.

But an immunity to the general ambiance of the neighbourhood can also cause more immediate feng shui problems.

Eyesore houses disturb the flow, upset the equilibrium of the land forms around them.

The attention is caught by these houses, but in a negative way, usually because whatever has been done is out of keeping with the surrounding environment. Often the colour or texture applied to the front of the house, or the plant life used in the garden, is so different from the rest of the area as to be almost alien. If a building causes you to flinch, be sure it will have the same effect on passing chi. Eyesore houses spoil the harmony of an area for everyone including, in the end, the owners themselves.

Learn from this and plan the front of your house accordingly:

- Take an **architectural interest** in vernacular materials and try to understand how and why they have been used in the area.
- Develop an eye for **local building shape** and structure. Gain some insight as to why roofs in your area are the angle they are, why windows open the way they do, why doors are the height they are and so on. Apply this understanding when making alterations or additions to your home, especially to the front.
- Observe **facades of other houses** in your street. Street

frontage is the contemporary interpretation of the Red Bird aspect in Form School feng shui; all the gardens joined together form a kind of Southern prairie. Therefore they should all have some commonality, even if it is simply a grassed area of some sort to the fore of the house.

This does not mean you should remonstrate with anyone in your street who is not conforming to Form School principles. Do your bit and rejoice in the knowledge that you are doing the right thing. Avoid priggishness though or you'll never convert anyone.

Consider your use of greenery, in particular be judicious in the planting of trees.

Look at the *appropriateness* of a tree in your garden. Will a tree enhance your neighbours' lives as well as your own? How will it affect light (both yours and theirs) in ten years' time? What about the roots – how far and how deep will they spread? And will you be able to *maintain* a tree, sweeping up leaves not just from your garden but your neighbours' and the pavement too. After all it's your tree, you're responsible for it, leaves and all. Lovely as they can be, a tree is a *commitment*. Be sure you want to devote the time and effort to one before you dig in.

Think about your front garden almost as a civic duty or community service.

The front of your house contributes to the quality of life of every individual who passes it. The effect may be fleeting or subconscious but the combined impact of a well-cared for and attractively presented street is incalculable. Sit quietly in your front room window one day and watch the people who pass your house. Children playing, dog-walkers, parents with prams, tootling motorists. Watch especially the elderly and see how much joy they extract from stopping and pointing and chatting about a particularly interesting garden feature or plant. **Don't forget people create chi too**. The better they feel, the more they use the street because they like to be there, **the greater the probability of good feng shui for those who live there**.

CHANGE OR MAINTAIN?

On the subject of trees, if you are gaining one along with the property and it is nor harmful or inconvenient to either you or your neighbours, think seriously before you remove it. Try even shifting it to another part of the garden before you cut it down.

- Old trees have a sense of stability, an established sort of energy which takes a new home and garden a long time to acquire.
- Old walls are the same. Lucky are the owners of a new house on old land who along with the bricks and mortar gain an ancient stone wall or well-established tree from the original property.

Let the place evolve around you for a while before taking any decisions about what should stay and what should go. Just keep it tidy and get to know the area. Have a look at the local landscape, what looks nice in other people's gardens and why. It might be that an attractive specimen is particularly suited to the local soil conditions or weather. Look at what currently thrives in your own garden (apart from the weeds).

In feng shui, indigenous is best. It works with the chi of the land.

By all means experiment with the exotic but not to the extent of denying yourself the benefits of the fauna and flora of your own locality. As a rule of thumb, if it struggles and has to be cosseted, its chi will generally be weak. If it's vigorous and healthy, the chi should be strong.

Beware also of **change for change's sake**. Consider carefully if planned alterations will actually result in an improvement to the property. Or is it simply a case of you, naturally enough, wanting to make your own stamp on the land as soon as possible? Perhaps to show yourself and others just whose house it is now?

Again, wait. Sometimes **moving into someone else's old house can feel a little intrusive**, as if we are a guest or visitor invading a stranger's home. Your new neighbours' initial and (again, quite understandable) apprehension about you will contribute to your feeling of being an outsider. They will be as unsure of you as you are of them.

- Give yourself and everyone else some time before imposing what might turn out to be quite unnecessary change on your new home.
- Get to know the people and the area before you make your mind up about how you are going to alter things.
- That idiosyncratic feature you have inherited in the front garden may actually have become an informal local landmark. Do you really want to change that? Live with it for a while. It might grow on you as it has on others.

③ GOING FOR COLOUR OR GREEN?

Gardens, like anything else, are a trade-off. What do you want – loadsa colour, lotsa work or minimal effort and a rather joyless little plot? Think differently. Your time may be limited but there are alternatives to a fully patioed-over front of house area. Work smarter, not harder.

First take into account what other people have done with the same amount of land in your vicinity. There's no need to accept wholesale someone else's taste but neither is there any point in reinventing the wheel. Concede good ideas when you see them and have the common sense to incorporate them in your own garden design. People do it all the time and they will do the same to you:

- **Go to garden centres** *in your area*. Look at what they are growing *outside* – away from cover. If it thrives there, so it should in your garden.

- **Ask advice** and **make friends**. People love to talk about their gardens. Let them and learn from them.

- **Don't lose sight** of the fact that you are trying to maintain a nod in the direction of **Form School feng shui**. Recall this when looking at paint colours and wall finishes. Do what you will to the back of your property but try to retain some **similarity to neighbouring properties** at the front. Think of the charming ice-cream colours of Brighton terraced houses and imagine what effect it would have if someone in the middle of a row painted their house magenta. Avoid such discord by blending in where possible.

- Having said that, if everyone else in the street has planted their borders with French marigolds and this isn't to your taste, don't feel obliged to copy them. You are attempting to **capture the *essence* of the area**, not emulate the whole thing.

- By all means paint your fence, fill pots and hang baskets. Before fitting ornamental shutters, however, look to see if anyone else in the street has them. The same goes for stone cladding, pebble dashing, velux windows. If they fit in, fine. Even then **consider if these innovations are really appropriate** to the **original design** of your home.

Year-round colour provided by trees, shrubs and flowers can be difficult to achieve but is worth the initial planning and investment to counteract the many grey days most of us experience during winter months.

- Colour can also be brought into the garden by the use of paint. Be sure the hues you are using **suit your surroundings** however.
- Consider the suitability and appropriateness of colour to the **weather conditions** and **general design** of your property.
- Note whether a **particular style** prevails. Or have things been drawn together from a variety of different sources?

Eclecticism is all well and good but if it's not done properly it can simply end up looking like an ill thought-out mess. This is particularly so in the use of **colour and texture**.

- Unless you live in a climate with continuously blazing sunshine, the multi-use of **primary colours** will simply make your home look like a children's nursery.
- On the other hand, **restrained shades** of ivy green and midnight navy, so in keeping with subtle British sunlight, can simply come over as flat and dull in a hot climate.
- Lots of things in the **same colour but different textures** can be very interesting and soothing.
- **Too many textures** in **too many colours** can have the opposite effect and become quite distracting. Look at the front of some houses and you will see a mixture of pink paving, black tarmac, concrete paths, wooden decking, terracotta tiles, pitch roof, painted wall, louvre

shutters, stained glass, frosted glass and wrought iron. All this and more – sometimes on one house. It's overwhelming. There is no harmony or balance. The energy is everywhere at once.

MAKING WHAT MATTERS WORK FOR YOU

✓ This is all about slipping in to your new property with the minimum of bother. Other people's opinions shouldn't really come into it, you might think, but surely you would prefer to get along with your neighbours than antagonise them? Wouldn't you prefer to live in a community where people considered each other and were there with support when it was needed?

✓ Feng shui is reciprocal. You project *and* receive chi, as does your home. Enhance your community by looking after your property. Your house is only one of many. Hit the right note and you will create harmony for yourself and everyone around you. Miss it and discord will be the result.

✓ The most obvious manifestation of your desire to fit in to a neighbourhood is the way you present your home. Even if people intellectually respect your right to a circa 1965 caravan on your front lawn, aesthetically and emotionally they will find it challenging and upsetting.

✓ Be guided by your environment. Change one thing at a time. Respect your neighbours' right to good feng shui and you automatically better your own.

7 Feng Shui in Action

A man travels the world over in search of what
he needs and returns home to find it. G. Moore

3 things that
really matter

1 **CREATING YOUR DREAM HOUSE**

2 **RECORDING CHANGES**

3 **KEEPING IT GOING**

To embrace feng shui is to heighten your awareness. To
implement feng shui properly you must do so with clarity
and intention. But it should not become a chore: it is more
a way of life. Before you can achieve what you want, it is
necessary to *know* what you want. Easier said than done;
most people don't know and often won't take the trouble to
find out. This section looks at **identifying what you want**
in terms of your new home, **recognising change** as it
occurs and **perpetuating that change in your life**.

① CREATING YOUR DREAM HOUSE

Everyone has an idea about the *feel* that they want to
achieve in their home, if not the actual look. The **feel of an
environment** includes not just what is visible and obvious
but also **the more subtle nuances** of what goes to make
up a home. Buy a large cuttings book and begin filling it
with examples of things which make up your idea of the
essence of the ideal home. If a book is too much trouble,

use a boxfile and simply put your bits and pieces inside it. Collect not only magazine and newspaper cuttings, but fabric swatches, paint samples, scraps of wool, metallic finishes, wood stains, pressed flowers, ribbons; in fact anything which builds up your picture of home – a poem, some music, a recipe for the first meal you'll make for friends, smells and aromas you find appealing, floor plans of where you'd like things to go. Anything and everything you like is acceptable.

Look through your box or book often. Leave it somewhere obvious so you can get to it easily. Encourage the family to contribute or make up a book or box for their own room. Think laterally. If you find a leaf in the colour you'd like to paint one of your rooms, put that in.

It's your dream; you can do what you like.

 RECORDING CHANGES

After you begin compiling ideas for your dream house buy a small pocket diary. Start to record **instances of change**. Every time you notice a **coincidence** in your life, record it in the diary. Do the same each time something happens when you might say to yourself 'That was lucky!' No matter how small or seemingly irrelevant the incident, record it. No need for a lot of narrative, just jot down the bones of what happened. After a period of three months or so look back over your entries. The results can be very interesting and often appear to form a pattern more often than not linked to the house.

③ KEEPING IT GOING

Feng shui is a lifetime commitment.

It is not a one-off treatment like plastic surgery, a nip for sagging spirits here, a tuck for improved luck there. It is more of an evolutionary improvement process, a way of **understanding and living**.

Feng shui is shaped to a large extent by our environment and as most of us change our environment on a day-to-day, often hour-by-hour basis, so the feng shui should be adjusted accordingly. The process is not static but ongoing, formed by our ever-altering circumstances.

Minding your feng shui should become second nature – instinct, in fact. And that's really what it's all about. **Providing the right balance of circumstances for instinct to flourish in order to allow that same instinct to benefit us**. Ultimately, feng shui helps us to control our lives and manifest our own luck.

> *Go, little book and wish to all*
> *Flowers in the garden, meat in the hall*
> *A bin of wine, a spice of wit*
> *A house with lawns enclosing it*
> *A living river by the door*
> *A nightingale in the sycamore*
> RLS

About the Author

Jane Purr is an established practitioner of feng shui in the classical tradition. Based in the North of England, she undertakes both domestic and commercial consultative work in feng shui as well as training in the subject. She also contributes to a variety of publications, TV and radio and speaks regularly to an array of different audiences. A background in management and personal development training, combined with a long-standing involvement with allied studies of vibrational energy underpin the professional methodology she uses in her day-to-day work in feng shui. Jane is an Associate of The Institute of Management (UK) and a Licentiate of The Institute of Personnel and Development (UK). She is also Northern Point of Contact for the UK Feng Shui Society.

Jane Purr can be contacted at: PO Box 80, Blaydon on Tyne, Tyne and Wear NE21 4YX. Tel/Fax: +44 – (0) 0191 4402276. E-mail: janepurr@clara.co.uk